ABAP Core Data Services

By Mark Anderson

Table of Contents

Introduction..4

    Structure of the Book..5

1.   Introduction to Core Data Services................................6

    1.1   What Is S/4HANA? 6

    1.2   ABAP Programming model in SAP S/4HANA 7

    1.3   Code Pushdown..9

    1.4   Core data services (CDS)................................10

    1.5   CDS View Templates 20

    1.6   Using a CDS View from an ABAP program 27

2.   CDS Data Modelling Concepts and Syntax................29

    2.1   Aggregate Expressions and Group By................29

    2.2   Having clause 31

    2.3   CASE Statements 32

    2.4   CAST Operations 33

    2.5   Support of SQL Functions 35

        2.5.1   Numeric Functions 35

        2.5.2   String Functions................................37

        2.5.3   Byte String Functions 39

        2.5.4   Coalesce Functions 40

    2.6   Support of Arithmetic Expressions 40

    2.7   Session Variables 41

    2.8   Client Handling 42

    2.9   Conversion for Currency and Quantity................43

        2.9.1   Currency Conversion 43

        2.9.2   Quantity Conversion 45

3.   Access Control..48

4.   CDS View Extension 51

5. Create a List Application with CDS views 54

   5.1   Create Interface and Consumption CDS views 56

   5.2   Activate and Maintain OData service 63

   5.3   Create UI5 project 66

Appendix 71

1. Installation of ABAP Development Toolkit 71

   1.1   Download and Install Eclipse 71

   1.2   Install the ABAP Development Tools for SAP NetWeaver (ADT) 72

   1.3   Connecting Eclipse to a Backend SAP System 73

Introduction

Over the last four decades SAP technology has evolved at a great speed.

SAP systems now touch 77% of the world's transactions and are the leading source of operational data like financials, customer transactions, supply chain, human resources, Insurance etc.

SAP's latest offering is S/4HANA, the next generation business suite. This is based on Core Data services (CDS), OData, BOPF etc.

CDS views can be described as the next generation database views and provides a full-fledged data model. Hence, CDS forms the nucleus(core) of the new ABAP programming model.

Hence, it goes without saying that now it is important for SAP developers to learn and master CDS.

The purpose of this book is to enable the inquisitive ABAP developers to learn the use of CDS views from the perspective of S/4HANA and understand its overall architecture.

Structure of the Book

The book is divided into five chapters. Each chapter focuses on a specific function and provides examples relating to it.

Chapter 1: Introduction to Core Data Services

This chapter introduces Code Data Services (CDS) Views and explains how the code pushdown works wonder for the performance of the applications. It also explains the best practices and the tools recommended to be used for developing applications in the S/4 Hana world.

Chapter 2: CDS Modelling concepts and Syntax

This chapter explains the CDS modelling concepts and syntax which are useful for defining data models.

Chapter 3: Access Control

This chapter explains the authorization concepts for accessing the data exposed by the CDS models.

Chapter 4: CDS View extension

Chapter 4 provides an overview of how the SAP delivered CDS views can be enhanced without modifications.

Chapter 5: Create a List Application with CDS Views

This chapter provides a step-by-step exercise on creation of CDS a list application with CDS Views.

1. Introduction to Core Data Services

Core Data Services (CDS) is a new data modelling infrastructure. With CDS, the data models are defined and consumed on the database rather than on the Application server. Hence, this helps in the code push down and drastically improves the performance.

This Chapter defines S/4HANA and then goes on to explain what is 'Code push down'. In this chapter we also see how we can create a CDS view using HANA Studio. As CDS views can be created/changed only in HANA studio and not in ABAP Workbench, it is a prerequisite to install HANA studio. The necessary steps to install HANA studio is provided in the Appendix of this book.

1.1 What Is S/4HANA?

SAP S/4HANA stands for SAP Business Suite for SAP HANA. It is a new product with a new code line for maximum leverage of SAP HANA. It is the next generation business suite and is built on advanced in-memory platform, SAP HANA, and offers a personalized user experience with SAP Fiori.

S/4HANA delivers massive simplifications (data model, user experience), innovations and offers personalized user experience with SAP Fiori.

SAP S/4HANA simplifies IT landscape and reduce cost of ownership (TCO), through:

- Reducing your data footprint.
- Working with larger data sets in one system saving hardware costs, operational costs, and time.

1.2 ABAP Programming model in SAP S/4HANA

The new ABAP programming model has been introduced with the ABAP release 7.50 SPS01, first only supporting the development of read-only Fiori apps, and then successively enhanced and improved with the following ABAP releases.

The new ABAP programming model is based on proven technologies such as Core Data Services (CDS) for the data modelling and access, OData protocol for the service exposure and the business object processing framework for the transactional processing.

The picture below gives an overview of the end-2-end stack:

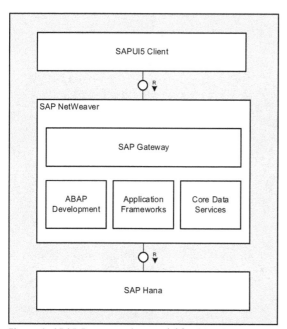

Figure 1: ABAP Programming model for SAP Fiori

SAPUI5: this is the latest UI technology from SAP and provides Role based access.

SAP Gateway: SAP Gateway is an open standards-based framework that developers can use to more easily connect non-SAP applications to SAP applications.

ABAP Development: New ABAP Language and Development tools.

Application Frameworks: One of the most important Application Frameworks used in S/4HANA is the Business Object Processing Framework (BOPF).

Core data Services: ABAP CDS provides a powerful data modelling infrastructure enabling advanced view building in the ABAP.

1.3 Code Pushdown

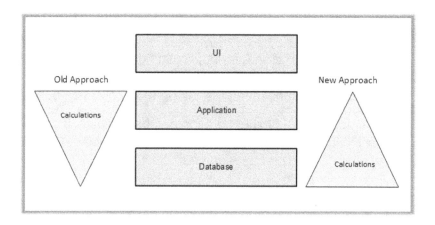

Figure 2: Code Push Down

With the brand-new NW AS ABAP 7.4 SP5, SAP is adding new possibility for ABAP Developers to leverage HANA capabilities.

Code pushdown means delegating data intense calculations to the database layer. It does not mean push ALL calculations to the database, but only those that make sense. An easy example is if you want to add the balances of a customer's saving account. You should not select all savings account balances and add them in your application logic code. This can be easily done by summing the account balances in the database and just return the result.

In ABAP programming, Developers were always expected to have a layered development approach i.e. keep the business logic separate from the data base access layer. This led to developers creating different Function Groups / Classes for Data base access and Application Logic. It might seem slightly strange that with Code pushdown we want to now put some Business logic in the database layer. But this is not new. Code pushdown was already being done in many ways like using Count (*) in Open SQL or by using Stored Procedures.

1.4 Core data services (CDS)

With the availability of SAP HANA there has been a shift in the way applications are developed. The idea is to push the code to the database layer to get maximum performance.

To take advantage of SAP HANA for application development, SAP introduced core data services. With CDS, data models are defined and consumed on the database rather than on the application server.

CDS views are nothing but next generation database views. It can be defined for an existing database table and any other views or CDS views. It uses Data Definition Language (DDL).

CDS is an infrastructure layer for defining semantically rich data models, which are represented as CDS views. CDS allows developers to define entity types (such as orders, business partners, or products) and the semantic relationships between them, which correspond to foreign key relationships in traditional entity relationship (ER) models.
CDS is defined using a SQL-based data definition language (DDL) that is based on standard SQL with some additional concepts, such as associations, which define the relationships between CDS views, and annotations, which direct the domain-specific use of CDS artifacts.

CDS data models go beyond the capabilities of the DDIC, which were typically limited to a transactional scope. For example, in CDS, you can define views that aggregate and analyze data in a layered fashion, starting with basic views and then adding powerful views that combine the basic views. Another difference is the support for special operators such as UNION, which enables the combination of multiple select statements to return only one result set.

1.4.1 CDS Views: A Step-by-Step Approach

The steps for developing with CDS views are as follows:
- Creating a CDS view
- Coding the CDS view
- Consuming the CDS view from ABAP code

Please note that traditional SE11 views were developed using forms which had tabs for selecting various configuration settings, definition of fields etc.
In CDS based approach the view is created using code.

STEP1: Start ABAP in Eclipse

DDL source (CDS views cannot be created in SE80).

To start ABAP in Eclipse, open the Eclipse project explorer and switch to the ABAP development perspective.

You can create these repository artifacts as local objects belonging to the $TMP package.
To create a CDS view, right click on the package and select New -> 'Other ABAP Repository Object'.

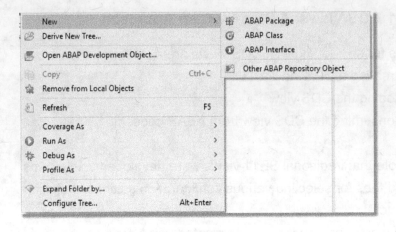

Figure 3: Create ABAP Repository Object

STEP2: Create a New CDS View

In the New ABAP Repository Object pop-up, search for the DDL source editor and select it to launch the New DDL Source wizard.

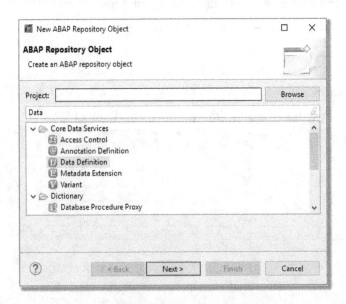

Figure 4: Create new CDS View

First, specify the basic properties of the view.

Enter a name of the view and its description.

In this example we will be creating a CDS view to select Business
Partners and its Default Addresses.

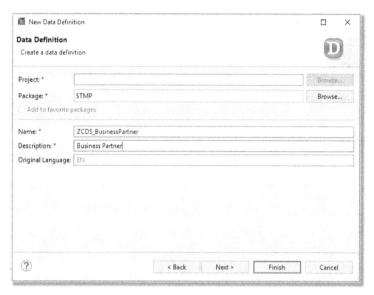

Figure 5: Create a Data Definition

Since we are creating the view as Local object the system does not
ask for a Transport request.

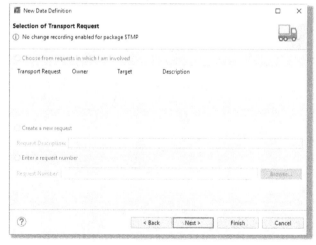

Figure 6: Select Transport Request

If the view were being created in an ABAP Package, then now the system would have prompted to specify a Transport Request number.

STEP3: Select a Template for the CDS View

The last screen of the New DDL Source wizard offers a selection of templates for creating a CDS view, including a display of the default syntax provided with each. The view can be created by either using one of the templates or without a template.

The templates include placeholders for code that you fill in step by step. If you later discover the need to change or extend the nature of your CDS view, you can always change the source code directly in the DDL editor and freely edit all parts of it as needed. This is particularly helpful if you want to copy portions of the source code from example code, for instance.

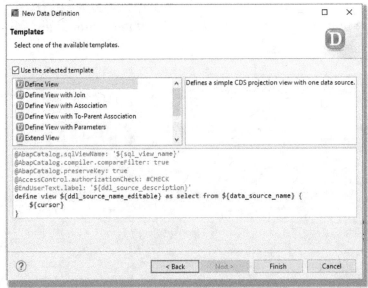

Figure 7: Select CDS Template

For our scenario we will create the view using the 'Define View with Association' template.

At this point let us understand the some of the frequently used templates.

- **Define View**: This can be used to read data from one table. This is like a select on a database table.

- **Define View with Join**: This is used to read data from more than one table. This is like a Select with Join to other tables. The table provides a template to join 2 tables, but this can be extended for more tables.

- **Define View with Association**: A View with Association is a type of join which is easier to write and understand.

- **Define View with Parameters**: CDS view can have parameters. The parameter values could be passed from the ABAP programs using the views.

- **Extend View**: This template is used when the CDS view is delivered by SAP and you want to extend the view with additional fields. E.g. SAP would provide a CDS view to read Business partner data. But this view could be extended with custom fields which you might have appended to the business partner table (BUT000).

STEP4: Complete the Coding for the View Definition

The code after having selected the Association template would look like as shown in the below figure:

```
@AbapCatalog.sqlViewName: 'sql_view_name'
@AbapCatalog.compiler.compareFilter: true
@AbapCatalog.preserveKey: true
@AccessControl.authorizationCheck: #CHECK
@EndUserText.label: 'Business Partner'
define view ZCDS_BusinessPartner as select from data_source_name
association [1] to target_data_source_name as _association_name
    on data_source_name.element_name = _association_name.target_element_name {

    _association_name // Make association public

}
```

Figure 8: CDS Sample Code

You would notice that there are various placeholders which needs to be filled.

Let us examine each of the lines in the above code.
The first few lines of the view starting with '@' are called Annotations. After the sign @ the annotation describes a specific behavior.

The first annotation requires us to specify the SQL view name. When we had created the CDS view, we had specified the name of the view. But this was the CDS view name.
Each DDL source has 2 names. The CDS view name and the SQL view name. The SQL view name is the name which can be used to see the view using SE11.

```
@AbapCatalog.sqlViewName: 'sql_view_name'
```

Replace the text 'sql_view_name' with 'zv_bus_part'. A SQL view name only allows 16 characters for the name as for a DDIC table / view.

The template has 4 more annotations. These are described below:

- `@AbapCatalog.compiler.compareFilter: true`

Defines the evaluation of filter conditions in path expressions of the CDS view

- @AbapCatalog.preserveKey: true

Specifies the definition of the key fields in the CDS database view of the CDS view.

- @AccessControl.authorizationCheck: #CHECK
  Defines implicit access control when Open SQL is used to access the CDS view.

  #CHECK:
  If Open SQL is used to access the view, access control is performed implicitly if a CDS role role is assigned to the view. If there is no role for the view, a syntax check warning occurs.

  #NOT_REQUIRED:
  Like #CHECK, but there is no syntax check warning.

  #NOT_ALLOWED:
  No access control is performed. This produces a syntax check warning in the DCL source code of a role for the view.

  #PRIVILEGED_ONLY:
  Privileged association (evaluated by SADL).

- @EndUserText.label: 'Business Partner'
  This is the description of the view which was specified when entering the attributes of the view.

Now specify the target data source for the Business Partner basic data. The underlying base table to be used as the target data source is named BUT000.

You can view the details of any of the syntactical elements that make up a CDS view definition on the fly by pressing the F2 key. The tooltip pop-up shows all the attributes, the corresponding data elements and types, and the associations (relationships) between the element and other tables or views, including their cardinality.

STEP 5: Add Associations details

While creating the view we had selected the template with associations as we wanted to select the default address of the Business partner.
We could create our own CDS view for default address or use the one delivered by SAP. In our example we will use the SAP BP Address CDS view (`I_BPCurrentDefaultAddress`).

The association could be added using the below code
association [0..1] to I_BPCurrentDefaultAddress   **as** _CurrentDefaultAddress   **on $projection**.BusinessPartner = _CurrentDefaultAddress.BusinessPartner

Please note that the association requires the following information

- Cardinality: This describes the number of records in the Default address table for the BP. Since is is possible to have either no or max 1 default address, the association is defined as [0..1]

- CDS view name: This is the CDS View name of the Second table i.e. Default address table.

- Association condition: This specifies the join condition between the CDS views.

The current code would look like as shown below

```
@AbapCatalog.sqlViewName: 'ZV_BUS_PART'
@AbapCatalog.compiler.compareFilter: true
@AbapCatalog.preserveKey: true
@AccessControl.authorizationCheck: #CHECK
@EndUserText.label: 'Business Partner'
define view ZCDS_BusinessPartner as select from but000
association [0..1] to I_BPCurrentDefaultAddress     as _CurrentDefaultAddress
                   on $projection.BusinessPartner = _CurrentDefaultAddress.BusinessPartner
    {

}
```

Figure 9: CDS Add annotation

STEP 6: Add the fields for the view

Now we should add the fields which for the view. E.g. We would like to return the business partner key, first name, last name.

The final code would look like below:

```
@AbapCatalog.sqlViewName: 'ZV_BUS_PART'
@AbapCatalog.compiler.compareFilter: true
@AbapCatalog.preserveKey: true
@AccessControl.authorizationCheck: #CHECK
@EndUserText.label: 'Business Partner'
define view ZCDS_BusinessPartner as select from but000
association [0..1] to I_BPCurrentDefaultAddress     as _CurrentDefaultAddress
        on $projection.BusinessPartner = _CurrentDefaultAddress.BusinessPartner
    {
    key    but000.partner                              as  BusinessPartner,
           but000.type                                 as  BusinessPartnerCategory,
           but000.augrp                                as  AuthorizationGroup,
           but000.partner_guid                         as  BusinessPartnerUUID,
           but000.persnumber                           as  PersonNumber,
           but000.name_first                           as  FirstName,
           but000.name_last                            as  LastName,

    _CurrentDefaultAddress // Make association public
}
```

Figure 10: CDS - Add components

Once the code is complete, we need to activate the View (just like a SE16 view).

STEP 7: Display the results

The Eclipse editor allows you to execute the CDS views and see the results.

The see the results, press the execute button

Figure 11: Execute CDS View

BusinessPartner	BusinessPartnerCategory	AuthorizationGroup	BusinessPartnerUUID	PersonNumber	FirstName	LastName
0000030500	1		047D7B8BFE3F1ED5B2CBF7F...	0000023252	Vendor ...	... for FAF
0100000197	1		047D7B8BFE3F1ED7AAB1557...	0000028439	Harry	Man
0100000106	1		047D7B8BFE3F1ED7889C3B1...	0000026509	CML	Training
7000000003	1		047D7B8BFE3F1ED7A7A1E16...	0000028051	USER31	ISUBP
0500000001	1		047D7B8BFE3F1EE6A8CE971...	0000024572	Good luck..	C4C
0100000119	1		047D7B8BFE3F1ED78AB0F94...	0000026647	Anand	Mehta
0100000022	2		047D7B8BFE3F1EE88BA9CEA...			
0100000067	2		047D7B8BFE3F1EE6A9B4A0D...			
0100000322	1		047D7B8BFE3F1EE8AFCF891...	0000030976		test
0900000012	2		047D7B8BFE3F1EE78AB62BC...			
0000030501	1		047D7B8BFE3F1EE5B2CEA30...	0000023256	Business Partner..	for FAF
0100000055	1		047D7B8BFE3F1EE69EE80FEC...	0000024348	test	C4C
0100000027	2		047D7B8BFE3F1EE68CFEC44...			
0100000038	2		047D7B8BFE3F1ED692B4862...			
0100000212	1		047D7B8BFE3F1ED7AD8F587...	0000028552	Supplier 01	01
0100000030	2		047D7B8BFE3F1EE6908CC01...			
0100000031	1		047D7B8BFE3F1EE6908CC48...	0000024067		
0100000034	2		047D7B8BFE3F1EE690E5FCA...			
0000000144	1		047D7B8BFE3F1EE690BA309...	0000024069	Test	RE-FX
0100000032	2		047D7B8BFE3F1EE690D31276...			
0100000041	1		047D7B8BFE3F1EE690E57A0...	0000024083	Deepthi	
0000000101	1		047D7B8BFE3F1EE690BA28F...	0000024068	Test	RE-FX
0000001201	2		047D7B8BFE3F1EE68BD8E8C...			
0100000035	2		047D7B8BFE3F1ED692B42E6...			
0100000026	1		047D7B8BFE3E1ED692B4562	0000024001	Dhyana	Ramkumar

Figure 12: Display results

1.5   CDS View Templates

In the previous section we created the CDS view with Association. In this section we will create CDS views with other commonly used templates and understand its usages with examples.

The following Templates will be covered:

- CDS View with Join
- CDS View with Parameters

1.5.1 CDS View with Join

CDS views with Joins are used for reading access to multiple Tables / Views. It might seem as if there is no difference between this View and the SE11 equivalent. But there are many differences. A CDS view allows outer joins – something that is not available in SE11 database views.

The following options are available:

- Combination of Several tables (JOIN):

    ○ **Inner Join**: One row of the left table and one row of the right table are always joined to a common result row - provided that the JOIN condition is fulfilled

    ○ **Left Outer join**: One row of a table and one row of another table are always connected to a common result row - provided that the JOIN condition is fulfilled. In addition, rows of the left table without matching row in the right table are copied to the query result. The missing values (from the right table) are filled with NULL values.

    ○ **Right Outer join**: One row of a table and one row of another table are always connected to a common result row - provided that the JOIN condition is fulfilled. In addition, rows of the right table without matching row in the left table are copied to the query result. The missing values (from the left table) are filled with NULL value.

    ○ **Full Outer Join**: One row of a table and one row of another table are always connected to a common result row - provided that the JOIN condition is fulfilled. In addition, rows of both tables without matching records are copied to the query result. The missing values (from the other table) are filled with NULL values.

- Combination of results of several sub-queries (UNION)
    ○ UNION ALL vs. UNION
        ▪ You can combine the result tables of multiple queries using UNION [ALL]. The individual

results tables must have the same number of columns. The corresponding result columns must have compatible data types.
If no name list specified, the column names of the result sets must match.

Let us create another CDS View with Joins. This time we will Create a View on the Business Partner table (BUT000) and Join it with Business Partner Role.

A CDS view with Join can be created using the Join Template.

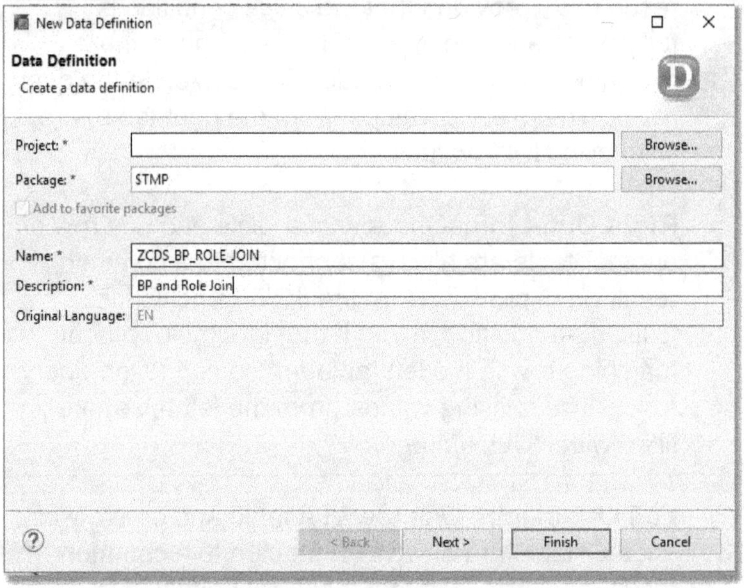

Figure 13: New Data Definition

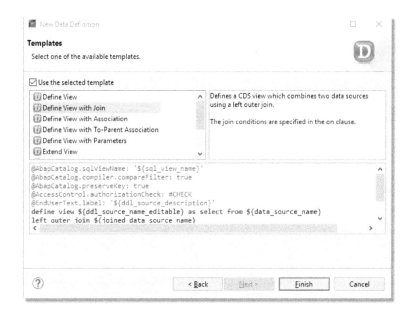

Figure 14: CDS - Select Template

The Generate code would be as shown below:

```
⊟ @AbapCatalog.sqlViewName: 'sql_view_name'
  @AbapCatalog.compiler.compareFilter: true
  @AbapCatalog.preserveKey: true
  @AccessControl.authorizationCheck: #CHECK
  @EndUserText.label: 'BP and Role Join'
  define view ZCDS_BP_ROLE_JOIN as select from data_source_name
  left outer join joined_data_source_name
      on data_source_name.element_name = joined_data_source_name.joined_element_name {

}
```

Figure 15: CDS - Sample Code

As in the previous example, do the following

- Provide an SQL View name
- Enter the data source names.
- Enter the Join Conditions
- Provide the Fields for selection

After completing the above steps, the code would look like as shown below

```
⊖ @AbapCatalog.sqlViewName: 'ZV_BP_ROLE'
  @AbapCatalog.compiler.compareFilter: true
  @AbapCatalog.preserveKey: true
  @AccessControl.authorizationCheck: #CHECK
  @EndUserText.label: 'BP and Role Join'
  define view ZCDS_BP_ROLE_JOIN as select from but000
  left outer join but100
    on but000.partner = but100.partner {
    key  but000.partner                         as  BusinessPartner,
         but000.type                            as  BusinessPartnerCategory,
         but000.augrp                           as  AuthorizationGroup,
         but000.partner_guid                    as  BusinessPartnerUUID,
         but000.persnumber                      as  PersonNumber,

         but100.rltyp                           as  BusinessPartnerRole
  }
```

Figure 16: CDS - Add Details

Execute the View and check the results

BusinessPartner	BusinessPartnerCategory	AuthorizationGroup	BusinessPartnerUUID	PersonNumber	BusinessPartnerRole
0000030500	1		047D7B8BFE3F1ED5B2CBF7...	0000023252	FLVN00
0100000197	1		047D7B8BFE3F1ED7AAB15...	0000028439	
0100000106	1		047D7B8BFE3F1ED7889C3B...	0000026509	TR0110
0100000106	1		047D7B8BFE3F1ED7889C3B...	0000026509	FLCU00
0100000106	1		047D7B8BFE3F1ED7889C3B...	0000026509	FLCU01
0100000106	1		047D7B8BFE3F1ED7889C3B...	0000026509	TR0100
7000000003	1		047D7B8BFE3F1ED7A7A1E1...	0000028051	MKK
0500000001	1		047D7B8BFE3F1EE6A8CE97...	0000024572	FLCU01
0100000119	1		047D7B8BFE3F1ED78AB0F9...	0000026647	TR0803
0100000022	2		047D7B8BFE3F1EE68BA9CE...		MKK
0100000022	2		047D7B8BFE3F1EE68BA9CE...		BBP000
0100000067	2		047D7B8BFE3F1EE6A9B4A0...		FLCU00
0100000067	2		047D7B8BFE3F1EE6A9B4A0...		FLCU01
0100000322	1		047D7B8BFE3F1EE8AFCF89...	0000030976	FLCU00
0900000012	2		047D7B8BFE3F1EE78AB62B...		FLVN00
0900000012	2		047D7B8BFE3F1EE78AB62B...		FLVN01
0000030501	1		047D7B8BFE3F1EE5B2CEA3...	0000023256	FLVN01
0000030501	1		047D7B8BFE3F1EE5B2CEA3...	0000023256	TR0803
0000030501	1		047D7B8BFE3F1EE5B2CEA3...	0000023256	TR0640
0000030501	1		047D7B8BFE3F1EE5B2CEA3...	0000023256	FLVN00
0000030501	1		047D7B8BFE3F1EE5B2CEA3...	0000023256	FLCU00
0000030501	1		047D7B8BFE3F1EE5B2CEA3...	0000023256	TR0600
0100000055	1		047D7B8BFE3F1EE69EE80FE...	0000024348	FLCU01
0100000027	2		047D7B8BFE3F1EE68CFEC4...		FLVN00

Figure 17: Display results

1.5.2 CDS View with Parameters

CDS views can be created with parameters which can be passed by the ABAP Programs.

e.g. you have a report with Selection screen. The user enters parameters on the screen and these parameters are directly passes to the CDS views to get the results.

The parameters are provided as Comma-Separated list with Type. The Types could be predefined type or Data elements.

These parameters could be used as ON conditions of JOINSs, Expressions in WHERE or HAVING clauses etc.

In a traditional SE16 view, the parameters used in Select can only be used to filter the result set, but here the parameters can be used anywhere in the CDS code.

Let us create a View with parameters to understand this View in more detail.

Example Scenario

Those who have already started working on S/4HANA would have faced an issue where they would have to access the F4 domain values to provide this as a Combo box in UI. This can be simplified by create a View which takes the Domain name as input, retrieves the domain values and returns the results.

To create the CDS view, create a new view and this time use the Template with Parameters.

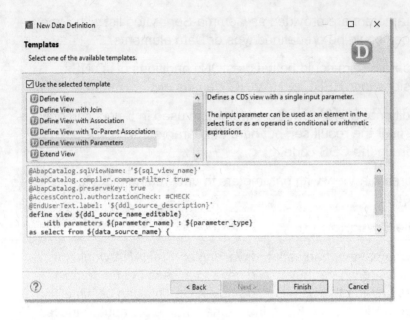

Figure 18: Select CDS View Parameter tempalte

Now replace the template code with the details

The final code should look like as shown below:

```
@AbapCatalog.sqlViewName: 'CheckWPDFIX'
@AbapCatalog.compiler.compareFilter: true
@AccessControl.authorizationCheck: #CHECK
@EndUserText.label: ' Value'

/*This CDS gives the domain values*/

define view C_Domnval_DomainFixedValues
  as select from    dd071 as value
    left outer join dd07t as text on  text.domname  = value.domname
                              and text.as4local = value.as4local
                              and text.as4vers  = value.as4vers
                              and text.valpos   = value.valpos
{
  key  value.domvalue_l,
//       @Semantics.text: true -- identifies the text field
       value.domvalue_h,
       value.domname,
       text.ddtext
}
where
       ddlanguage      = $session.system_language
  and value.as4local = 'A'
}
```

Figure 19: CDS View with Parameters

Now activate and execute the view.

This time, the system does not display the results directly. It asks for the parameter value and then displays the results.

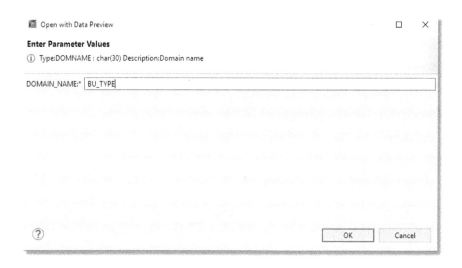

Figure 20: Enter Input values

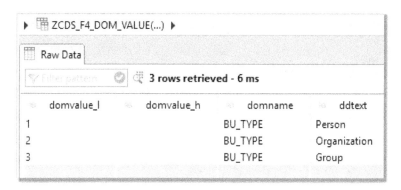

Figure 21: Display results

1.6 Using a CDS View from an ABAP program

CDS Views are used in the same way as the classical SE16 views. You could use the views in Select statements.

```
SELECT * FROM zcds_businesspartner INTO TABLE @DATA(lt_b
p).
```

Please note that when using the CDS view we specify the CDS view name and not the SQL name.

SUMMARY

This chapter introduced you to CDS View and explained some of the commonly used Templates. With the details covered in this chapter you should not be comfortable in creating different views and exposing the data to the calling applications.

2. CDS Data Modelling Concepts and Syntax

2.1 Aggregate Expressions and Group By

CDS provides aggregate expressions which can be used to calculate single value from multiple rows of a results set by calling an aggregate function.

The following table shows the possible aggregate functions:

Aggregate Expression	Description
MIN	Returns the smallest value in operand
MAX	Returns the greatest value in operand
SUM	Calculates the sum of the values of operand
AVG	Calculates the average value of the values of operand
COUNT(*)	Returns the number of entries in the result set
COUNT(DISTINCT operand)	Returns the number of distinct values of operand

To understand this better let us take the example of Sales Orders. For our example, we will create a CDS view to select data from Sales Order Item table. This table contains one or more Sales order items for a Sales Order.

To use the Aggregate functions, we will use the 'GROUP BY' clause to group the items of the same Sales Order together. The aggregate functions will act on the list of Sales order items belonging to the same Sales Order header and provide the result.

```
@AbapCatalog.sqlViewName: 'ZISALESORD1'
@AbapCatalog.compiler.compareFilter: true
@AbapCatalog.preserveKey: true
@AccessControl.authorizationCheck: #CHECK
@EndUserText.label: 'Sales Order header'
define view ZI_SalesOrd1
  as select from vbap
{
```

```
key vbeln          as SalesDocument,
min(netwr)         as MinAmount,
max(netwr)         as MaxAmount,
avg(netwr)         as AvgAmount,
count(*)           as ItemCount,
count(distinct matnr) as DistinctMaterial

} group by vbeln
```

On executing the above CDS view the data preview would be like as shown below:

SalesDocument	MinAmount	MaxAmount	AvgAmount	ItemCount	DistinctMaterial
0000000038	10.00	10.00	1.00000000000...	1	1
0000000039	100.00	100.00	1.00000000000...	1	1
0000000040	0.00	20.00	7.50000000000...	4	2
0000000041	100.00	100.00	1.00000000000...	1	1
0000000042	100.00	100.00	1.00000000000...	1	1
0000000043	100.00	150.00	1.25000000000...	2	2
0000000044	100.00	150.00	1.25000000000...	2	2
0000000045	100.00	100.00	1.00000000000...	1	1

Figure 22: Data preview - Aggregate functions

Let us now analyze the above result with the Sales Order number '0000000040'.

The data in the table VBAP for this Sales Order as follows:

Data Browser: Table VBAP Select Entries   4

🖉 🔍 🛎 ▽ 🗐 🗋 ⏏ ⓘ Check Table...

Table: VBAP
Displayed Fields: 5 of   5   Fixed Columns: [3]   List Width 0250

MANDT	VBELN	POSNR	MATNR	NETWR
001	0000000040	000010	CBC-1	10,00
001	0000000040	000020	SAMPLE	20,00
001	0000000040	000030	SAMPLE	0,00
001	0000000040	000040	SAMPLE	0,00

- Sales Order has 4 Sales order items.
- The Sum of the new Price of all the item is 30 (10 + 20).
- The average value of the net price for 4 items is 30/4 = 7.5.
- The Sales order has 2 distinct materials (CBC-1 and SAMPLE).

- The minimum Value of Net Price is 0 and the Maximum is 20.

As you would have noticed the expected results match with the results shown in the data preview.

2.2 Having clause

The HAVING clause defines a HAVING condition for the results set of a CDS view after a GROUP BY clause is evaluated.
A HAVING condition can only be specified together with GROUP BY.

The HAVING clause removes all rows from the results set that do not meet the condition 'cond_expr' specified after HAVING.

Let us take the previous example used in aggregate functions. If we want to have a result set where the Sales Order item Category (pstyv) = 'TAN', then the query would be as shown below.

```
@AbapCatalog.sqlViewName: 'ZISALESORD1'
@AbapCatalog.compiler.compareFilter: true
@AbapCatalog.preserveKey: true
@AccessControl.authorizationCheck: #CHECK
@EndUserText.label: 'Sales Order header'
define view ZI_SalesOrd1
  as select from vbap
{
  key vbeln         as SalesDocument,
  min(netwr)        as MinAmount,
  max(netwr)        as MaxAmount,
  avg(netwr)        as AvgAmount,
  count(*)          as ItemCount,
  count(distinct matnr) as DistinctMaterial

} group by vbeln, pstyv
  having pstyv = 'TAN'
```

The data preview for the result is as shown below:

Filter pat... 100 rows retrieved - 52 ms (partial result) SQL Console | Data Aging | Num

SalesDocument	MinAmount	MaxAmount	AvgAmount	ItemCount	DistinctMaterial
0000000037	0.00	0.00	0.00000000000...	1	1
0000000025	400.00	400.00	4.00000000000...	1	1
0000000058	10.00	10.00	1.00000000000...	1	1
0000000062	1000.00	2000.00	1.50000000000...	2	1
0000000063	0.00	0.00	0.00000000000...	2	2
0000000064	0.00	0.00	0.00000000000...	2	2

Figure 23: Data preview: HAVING clause

Let us analyze the result for Sales order number '000000025'.

The data preview shows that the item count is 1 and it has 1 distinct material. The table in the database however has 2 entries.

Data Browser: Table VBAP Select Entries 2

Check Table...

Table: VBAP
Displayed Fields: 6 of 6 Fixed Columns: 3 List Width 0250

MANDT	VBELN	POSNR	MATNR	PSTYV	NETWR
001	0000000025	000010	M-0001	TANN	0,00
001	0000000025	000020	M-0001	TAN	400,00

Figure 24: Sample Sales order item data in table

One of the entries (Item number 00010) was removed due to the HAVING clause (pstyv <> 'TAN').

2.3 CASE Statements

Case statements provide decision making capabilities to the CDS views. Case statements can also be nested.

Case statements can be used to return different values as output for the view based on the data of the underlying artifact.

```
@AbapCatalog.sqlViewName: 'ZISALESORD1'
@AbapCatalog.compiler.compareFilter: true
@AbapCatalog.preserveKey: true
@AccessControl.authorizationCheck: #CHECK
@EndUserText.label: 'Sales Order header'
```

```
define view ZI_SalesOrd1
  as select from vbak
{
  key vbeln as SalesDocument,
      erdat as RecordDate,
      erzet as Entrytime,
      case  vbtyp
      when 'C' then 'Order'
      when 'A' then 'Enquiry'
      else 'Other Doc types'
      end   as DocCategory

}
```

In the above example, the SD document category (vbtyp) is evaluated by the case statement to return more user understandable description.

The output of the above code would be as shown below:

SalesDocument	RecordDate	Entrytime	DocCategory
0000000600	2019-08-11	06:48:39 PM	Order
0010000000	2016-09-27	01:22:18 PM	Enquiry
0020000001	2016-09-27	01:52:08 PM	Other Doc types
0000000200	2017-11-17	06:38:08 AM	Order
0020000002	2016-09-27	01:59:42 PM	Other Doc types
0000000215	2018-02-14	02:55:52 AM	Order
0020000003	2016-10-19	11:59:17 AM	Other Doc types
0020000004	2016-10-20	07:28:41 AM	Other Doc types
0020000005	2016-10-20	07:30:43 AM	Other Doc types

ZI_SALESORD1

Raw Data

100 rows retrieved - 21 ms (partial result)

Figure 25: Data preview Case statement

2.4 CAST Operations

Cast operations can be used for determining the type of the calculated field or for converting the type of the existing fields on the database level.

The following can be specified for **data type**

- Any data element. In this case, the optional addition PRESERVING TYPE can be specified. If this addition is specified, the built-in data type, the length of the operand and the number of decimal places, and the target data type must match exactly.
- A built-in data type in ABAP Dictionary. The addition PRESERVING TYPE cannot be specified in this case.

```
@AbapCatalog.sqlViewName: 'ZISALESORD1'
@AbapCatalog.compiler.compareFilter: true
@AbapCatalog.preserveKey: true
@AccessControl.authorizationCheck: #CHECK
@EndUserText.label: 'Sales Order header'
define view ZI_SalesOrd1
  as select from vbak
{
  key vbeln        as SalesDocument,
      cast(erdat as abap.char( 8 ))        as RecordDate

}
```

In the above sample code, the field SalesDocument assumes the same type as the field vbeln. Casting for the erdat field converts the values of the field (which is of type dats) into a character of length 8. Hence, the field RecordDate is a character string of length 8.

The list of types that can be used for casting is described in the below table:

Data Type	Description
abap.char(len)	CHAR with length len
abap.clnt[(3)]	CLNT
abap.cuky(len)	CHAR with length len
abap.curr(len,decimals)	CURR with length len and decimals decimal places
abap.dats[(8)]	DATS
abap.dec(len,decimals)	DEC with length len and decimals decimal places

abap.fltp[(16,16)]	FLTP
abap.int1[(3)]	INT1
abap.int2[(5)]	INT2
abap.int4[(10)]	INT4
abap.int8[(19)]	INT8
abap.lang[(1)]	LANG
abap.numc(len)	NUMC with length len
abap.quan(len,decimals)	QUAN with length len with decimals decimal places
abap.raw(len)	RAW
abap.sstring(len)	SSTRING
abap.tims[(6)]	TIMS
abap.unit(len)	CHAR with length len

2.5 Support of SQL Functions

CDS Views offer various built-in SQL functions which eases the work of a developer.

The possible functions are:

- Numeric functions
- String functions
- Byte String functions
- Coalesce functions

Numeric Functions

The following table shows the possible numerical SQL functions in a CDS view.

FUNCTION	DEFINITION	OUTPUT
ABS(arg)	In mathematics, the absolute value or modulus |x| of a real number x is the non-negative value of x without regard to its sign	Absolute amount
CEIL(arg)	Hitting the Ceiling of	Smallest integer

	the Floating Number.	number not less than the value of arg
DIV(arg1, arg2)	Conventional Division	Quotient
DIVISION(arg1, arg2, dec)	Conventional Division but with an additional feature of specificing deicmal places	The result is rounded to dec decimal places.
MOD(arg1, arg2)	Conventional Modulo Operation	Remainder
FLOOR(arg)	Largest integer number not greater than the value of arg.	More like scientific numbers
ROUND(arg, pos)	Rounded value of arg.	Rounding the Designated decimal point value

Let us understand the functions with the help of the below sample code.

```
@AbapCatalog.sqlViewName: 'ZISDAQL'
@AbapCatalog.compiler.compareFilter: true
@AbapCatalog.preserveKey: true
@AccessControl.authorizationCheck: #CHECK
@EndUserText.label: 'SQL Functions'
define view zi_sd_sql_functions
  as select from vbak
{
// Sales document numer
  vbak.vbeln                as Sales_Doc,
// Net Price
  vbak.netwr                as Net_Price,
//Rounding of net price to 1 decimal place
  round(vbak.netwr,1)       as Round_Op,
// Ceiling of Net Price
  ceil(vbak.netwr)          as Ceil_Price,
// Floor of Net Price
  floor(vbak.netwr)         as Floor_Price,
// Divide net price by 3
  div(vbak.netwr,3)         as Div_Op,
// Divide net price by 3 with the result rounded to 5
decimal places
  division(vbak.netwr,3,5) as Div_Op2,
//Remainder operation
  mod(10,3)                 as Mod_Op,
// Fixed Absolute value
```

```
    abs(-10)                          as Abs_Op

}
```

When the above code is executed the result is as follows:

Sales_Doc	Net_Price	Round_Op	Ceil_Price	Floor_Price	Div_Op	Div_Op2	Mod_Op	Abs_Op
0000000025	400.00	400.00	400	400	133	133.33333	1	10
0000000006	0.00	0.00	0	0	0	0.00000	1	10
0000000600	4012.55	4012.60	4.013	4012	1337	1337.51667	1	10
0010000000	0.00	0.00	0	0	0	0.00000	1	10
0020000001	100.00	100.00	100	100	33	33.33333	1	10
0000000200	0.00	0.00	0	0	0	0.00000	1	10

Figure 26: Numerical SQL functions sample code output

2.5.2 String Functions

Several String functions can be used in CDS views. The list is provided in the table below. These functions are directly executed in the DB level.

Function	Description
Length	gives Length of String
Instr	finds the position of respective string within corresponding the field of the View
Concatenate	joining two strings
Concatenate with Space	Third Parameter in this function represents the Number of space between two strings
Left	gives us left most characters equal to argument passed
Lower	converts all into lower case [Rather Subscript]
Lpad & Rpad	first parameter is field, second is the OUTPUT Length after padding, string that is to be padded
Ltrim & Rtrim	first parameter is field, second is string or character that is to be

	removed
Replace	second parameter finds the string to be replaced by the third
Substring	finds the string that you want – second parameter is starting position and third is how many characters
Upper	converts all characters of string into Upper case

Sample code for executing some of the string functions is provided below:

```
@AbapCatalog.sqlViewName: 'ZIPRSTRFUNC'
@AbapCatalog.compiler.compareFilter: true
@AbapCatalog.preserveKey: true
@AccessControl.authorizationCheck: #CHECK
@EndUserText.label: 'String Functions'
define view zi_pr_string_fun
  as select from eban
{
  // PR Number
  banfn                    as PR_Num,
  // PR Short Text
  txz01                    as PR_Description,
  // PR Short Text in Upper Case
  upper( txz01 )           as Text_upper,
  //left most characters equal to argument passed
  left( txz01, 5 )         as Text_left,
  //
  rpad( txz01, 8, 'y' )    as Text_rpad,
  //Substring of the description
  substring( txz01, 2, 3 ) as Text_substring

}
```

▤ Raw Data

| | ✓ ◈ 100 rows retrieved - 22 ms (partial result) | | | | ◈ SQL Console | Data Aging | *n* Nu |

PR_Num	PR_Description	Text_upper	Text_left	Text_rpad	Text_substring
0010000118	Test	TEST	Test	Testyyyy	est
0010000120	PRR CODE 08/15 (2)	PRR CODE 08/15 (2)	PRR C	PRR CODE	RR
0010000120	PRR CODE 08/15	PRR CODE 08/15	PRR C	PRR CODE	RR
0010000121	PRR CODE 08/15	PRR CODE 08/15	PRR C	PRR CODE	RR
0010000121	PRR CODE 08/15 (2)	PRR CODE 08/15 (2)	PRR C	PRR CODE	RR
0010000181	Testmaterial SC	TESTMATERIAL SC	Testm	Testmate	est
0010000237	Soyabeans	SOYABEANS	Soyab	Soyabean	oya
0010000253	Sam Test 12345	SAM TEST 12345	Sam T	Sam Test	am

The resulting output is as shown below:

Analysis:

- The string function UPPER converts the PR description text into upper case. This can be seen in the column Text_upper.

- The function LEFT extracts part of the string. In the example scenario the argument for the number of characters was 5. Hence, left most 5 characters are extracted for output.

- The RPAD function adds the character 'y' (passed as argument) whenever the length of the text is less than 8 characters. It converts the text less than 8 characters to a string of 8 characters by padding the character 'y' to the right.

- The function SUBSTRING extracts a part of the string. In our case we have extracted 3 characters starting from the 2nd character.

2.5.3 Byte String Functions

The following table shows the possible SQL functions for byte strings in a CDS view.

- **BINTOHEX**: Converts a binary value to a hexadecimal value as a VARCHAR data type. If the input value is not a binary value, then it is first converted to a binary value.

The following example converts the binary value AB to a hexadecimal VARCHAR value 4142:

```
SELECT BINTOHEX('AB') "bintohex" FROM DUMMY;
```

- **HEXTOBIN**: HEXTOBIN returns a VARBINARY value where each byte of the result corresponds to two characters of *<hexadecimal_string>*. If *<hexadecimal_string>* does not contain an even number of digits, an error is returned.

The following two examples return the VARBINARY value 608DA975:

```
SELECT HEXTOBIN ('608da975') "Result" FROM DUMMY;
```

2.5.4 Coalesce Functions

Coalesce function in a SELECT statement of a CDS view. The coalesce function returns the value of the argument arg1 (if this is not the null value); otherwise it returns the value of the argument arg2. The arguments can be literals, fields of a data source, input parameters, predefined functions, or expressions of data types CHAR, SSTR, CLNT, LANG, NUMC, CUKY, UNIT, DATS, TIMS, FLTP, DEC, CURR, QUAN, INT1, INT2, or INT4 or INT8.

The data types of both arguments must either match or the data type of one argument must represent the full value of the other data type. The result has the dictionary type of the argument with the greater value range.

2.6   Support of Arithmetic Expressions

CDS Views support Addition, Subtraction, Multiplication and Division operations. Division is only possible for floating numbers.

Sample code is as shown below:

```
@AbapCatalog.sqlViewName: 'ZISALESORD1'
@AbapCatalog.compiler.compareFilter: true
@AbapCatalog.preserveKey: true
@AccessControl.authorizationCheck: #CHECK
@EndUserText.label: 'Sales Order header'
define view ZI_SalesOrd1
  as select from vbak
{
  key vbeln          as SalesDocument,
      erdat          as RecordDate,
      erzet          as Entrytime,
      netwr          as NetValue,
      cast( netwr as abap.fltp(16) ) *  0.3 as TaxAmount

}
```

The Net price (netwr) is multiplied with 0.3 to calculate the tax amount and the result is part of the column TaxAmount.

▸ ⁀ ZI_SALESORD1 ▸

⊞ Raw Data

	100 rows retrieved - 3 ms (partial result)			⊞ SQL Console	Da

SalesDocument	RecordDate	Entrytime	NetValue	TaxAmount
0000000434	2019-06-06	06:06:08 AM	11000.00	3.3000000000000005E+03
0000000381	2019-03-06	09:34:59 AM	20.00	6.0000000000000009E+00
0000000455	2019-06-08	05:27:58 PM	0.00	0.0000000000000000E+00
0000000235	2018-06-18	12:28:25 PM	20.00	6.0000000000000009E+00
0000000025	2017-04-03	09:46:13 AM	400.00	1.2000000000000001E+02
0000000006	2016-08-11	03:28:51 PM	0.00	0.0000000000000000E+00
0000000600	2019-08-11	06:48:39 PM	4012.55	1.2037650000000003E+03

Figure 27: Arithmetic expressions sample code output

2.7 Session Variables

CDS framework provides some runtime system variables which can be readily used to make CDS more optimal and feature-rich.

- **$session.user** is the current user name (same as sy-uname).
- **$session.client** is runtime SAP client which is equivalent to sy-mandt.
- **$session.system_date** is current system date and works same as sy-datum.
- **$session.system_language** is the language of the current text environment (same as sy-langu).

2.8 Client Handling

For CDS views you use the annotation **@CLientHandling** in order to define the client dependency and how client handling is done internally. For that you can specify the following two sub annotations:

```
@ClientHandling.type: #INHERITED | #CLIENT_DEPENDENT | #CLIENT_INDEPENDENT
```

Determines the client dependency.

- With the value #INHERITED (default), the client dependency of the view is determined by the data sources used. If one of the data sources used in the view is client dependent, the view is client dependent. If none of the data sources used in the view is client dependent, the view is client independent.
- With the value #CLIENT_DEPENDENT the view is client dependent. At least one of the data sources must be client dependent.
- With the value #CLIENT_INDEPENDENT the view is client independent. None of the data sources can be client dependent.

```
@ClientHandling.algorithm #AUTOMATED | #SESSION_VARIABLE | #NONE
```

Determines the client handling.

- If the value #AUTOMATED (default for client dependent views) is specified, the *ON* conditions of the view and other clauses are implicitly extended by conditions for the client columns of the underlying data sources.
- If the value #SESSION_VARIABLE is specified, additionally to the above extensions implicit *WHERE* conditions are added, that select the client that is currently stored in the session variable **$session.client**. During an Open SQL access this session variable contains the current client or the one set by the *USING CLIENT* addition. The result is the same as for #AUTOMATED but the performance can be better.
- The value #NONE is possible for client independent views only and it is their default.

If you don't specify @CLientHandling explicitly, it is the same as

@ClientHandling.type:#INHERITED
@ClientHandling.algorithm:#AUTOMATED

A client-specific CDS view has no client column. If you use Open SQL *SELECT* to access a client-specific CDS view, the data of the current client or the client specified in the addition *USING CLIENT* is read implicitly.

2.9 Conversion for Currency and Quantity

The CDS syntax allows you to embed conversion functions directly into the implementation of your CDS views.

Currency Conversion

Currency conversion has 4 mandatory parameters + 6 optional parameters to support fine adjustments in the output, client verification and error handling. The specification is available below:

Formal Parameter	Optional	Data Type
amount	–	CURR

source_currency	–	CUKY
target_currency	–	CUKY
exchange_rate_date	–	DATS
exchange_rate_type	X	CHAR with length 4
client	X, –	CLNT
round	X	CHAR
decimal_shift	X	CHAR
decimal_shift_back	X	CHAR
error_handling	X	CHAR with length 20

Let us now look at an example where we will convert the price from the Purchase requisition table.

```
@AbapCatalog.sqlViewName: 'ZIPRQUANCON'
@AbapCatalog.compiler.compareFilter: true
@AbapCatalog.preserveKey: true
@AccessControl.authorizationCheck: #CHECK
@EndUserText.label: 'Price conversion'
define view zi_pr_quan_conv
 with parameters p_DispCurr : waers_curc
  as select from eban
{
  key banfn,
  key bnfpo,
      @Semantics.amount.currencyCode: 'TransCurrency'
      preis,
      @Semantics.currencyCode: true
      waers as TransCurrency,

      badat as ReqDate,

      @Semantics.amount.currencyCode: 'DisplayCurr'
      currency_conversion( amount => preis,
                           source_currency => waers,
                           target_currency => :p_DispCurr,
                           exchange_rate_date => badat

                         )
      as DispAmount,

      @Semantics.currencyCode: true
      :p_DispCurr as DisplayCurr

}
```

In this example, we are converting the price in Purchase requisition (preis) to a price in another currency. The target currency is passed to the CDS view as a parameter (p_DispCurr). The function used to convert the currency is `currency_conversion.`

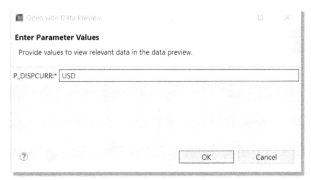

Figure 28: Input Traget currency as a parameter

The resultant output is a shown in the below listing.

▸ 🗂 ZI_PR_QUAN_CONV(...) ▸

🔲 Raw Data

✅ 🖳 **100 rows retrieved - 62 ms (partial result)**	⇨ Parameter	⌨ SQL Console	Data Aging

banfn	bnfpo	preis	TransCurrency	ReqDate	DispAmount	DisplayCurr
00100000...	00010	425.00	EUR	2016-03-10	399.50	USD
00100002...	00010	24.00	EUR	2019-06-07	26.78	USD
00100000...	00020	11000.00	EUR	2017-04-24	10340.00	USD
00100000...	00010	1000.00	EUR	2017-04-26	940.00	USD
00100000...	00020	1560.00	EUR	2017-04-26	1466.40	USD
00100000...	00030	12100.00	EUR	2017-04-26	11374.00	USD
00100000...	00010	0.00	EUR	2017-05-02	0.00	USD
00100000...	00010	0.00	EUR	2017-05-02	0.00	USD
00100000...	00010	1000.00	EUR	2017-05-03	940.00	USD

Figure 29: Currency Conversion sample code output

2.9.2 Quantity Conversion

Unit conversion has 3 mandatory parameters + 2 optional parameters to support client verification and error handling. The specification is available below:

Formal Parameter	Optional	Data Type
quantity	–	QUAN, DEC, INT1, INT2, INT4, FLTP
source_unit	–	UNIT
target_unit	–	UNIT
client	X, –	CLNT
error_handling	X	CHAR with length 20

Let us try the quantity conversion with the below sample code. In the example we will convert the quantity of a material from Base unit of Measure to a different Unit.

```
@AbapCatalog.sqlViewName: 'ZIPRQUANCON'
@AbapCatalog.compiler.compareFilter: true
@AbapCatalog.preserveKey: true
@AccessControl.authorizationCheck: #CHECK
@EndUserText.label: 'Price Quantity conversion'
define view zi_pr_quan_conv
  as select from mara
{
  key matnr as Material, //Purchase Requisition Number

      @Semantics.quantity.unitOfMeasure: 'SourceUnit'
      brgew as MaterialQuan,

      @Semantics.unitOfMeasure: true
      meins as SourceUnit,

      @Semantics.quantity.unitOfMeasure: 'DispUnit'
      unit_conversion( quantity     => brgew,
                       source_unit => meins,
                       target_unit => gewei
                     )
      as ConvQuantity,

      @Semantics.unitOfMeasure: true
      gewei as DispUnit

}
```

```
where matnr = '0000000000220000025'
```

The result of the above sample code would be as follows:

Figure 30: Quantity conversion sample code output

3. Access Control

As you would have already understood, CDS views are used to read the data and is used to expose the data (via OData) to the outside world. Hence, it is required to have a control mechanism so that only authorized users have access to the data. This is possible with the use of data control language (DCL).

ABAP Core Data Services (CDS) has its own authorization concept based on a data control language (DCL). The authorization concept of ABAP CDS uses conditions defined in CDS and can draw upon classical (PFCG) authorizations to check the authorizations of users.

The CDS authorization concept coexists with the classical authorization concept of SAP NetWeaver Application Server for ABAP (SAP NetWeaver AS for ABAP). You can use the concepts together or independently from another. The classical authorization concept is based on authorization objects. The authorization of a user occurs either implicitly, for example while calling a transaction, or explicitly with the statement AUTHORITY-CHECK. The CDS authorization concept is based on implicit authorization checks that occur during access attempts to CDS entities over service adaptation definition language (SADL) or Open SQL.

You might have noticed the annotation for authorization check in the previous sections.

```
@AccessControl.authorizationCheck: #CHECK
```

In this DCL approach, the authorization checks are executed as part of the view. Hence a CDS view is not only the DDL but it also includes DCL.

Let us assume that we want to create a DCL for the previously created CDS View (the one which displays the BP data).

```
@AbapCatalog.sqlViewName: 'ZV_BUS_PART'
@AbapCatalog.compiler.compareFilter: true
@AbapCatalog.preserveKey: true
@AccessControl.authorizationCheck: #CHECK
@EndUserText.label: 'Business Partner'
define view ZCDS_BusinessPartner as select from but000
association [0..1] to I_BPCurrentDefaultAddress     as _CurrentDefaultAddress
       on $projection.BusinessPartner = _CurrentDefaultAddress.BusinessPartner
    {
    key    but000.partner                                 as  BusinessPartner,
           but000.type                                    as  BusinessPartnerCategory,
           but000.augrp                                   as  AuthorizationGroup,
           but000.partner_guid                            as  BusinessPartnerUUID,
           but000.persnumber                              as  PersonNumber,
           but000.name_first                              as  FirstName,
           but000.name_last                               as  LastName,

    _CurrentDefaultAddress // Make association public
}
```

To create a DCL create an Access Control object, select Access Control while creating the view.

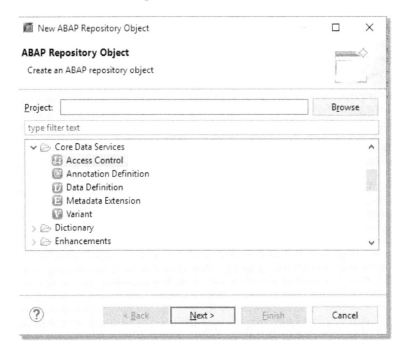

Figure 25: Create Access Control

Enter the below code

```
@EndUserText.label: 'BP authorization'
@MappingRole: true
define role Zbp_Auth {
    grant
        select
            on
                ZCDS_BusinessPartner
                    where ( AuthorizationGroup) ?=
                    aspect pfcg_auth (  B_BUPA_GRP,
                        BEGRU,
                        actvt = '03' )
                    ;

}
```

This DCL code is executed whenever a user tries to access data
from the CDS view. If the user does not have access to the
authorization object, then the data is not returned.

Guidelines

- The DCL document must include the annotation
  @MappingRole: true.
- Only one mapping role definition per DCL source document is
  allowed.
- Other aspects than pfcg_auth shall not be used.
- Only one mapping role per CDS view is allowed.

A DCL source document shall always include the mapping for one
CDS view exclusively i.e. a DCL cannot belong to more than 1 DDL.

4. CDS View Extension

SAP customers need to extend SAP delivered tables/Views with Customer fields for their custom requirements.

E.g. An airline company would extend the business partner table to store the food preferences of its customers. Hence, the table BUT000, which stores the Business Partner data, should be extended with new fields.

Hence, it should be possible to extend the SAP delivered CDS views with the custom fields as well so that this can be exposed to the UI. SAP provides this capability and the CDS views can be enhanced with additional fields, arithmetic & case expressions and literals.

These extensions are stored and transported in separate DDL source.

Let us see how this works with the Business Partner example.

SAP delivers a CDS view I_BusinessPartner, which selects data from the table but000.

Let us know extend this table by adding a custom field as shown below:

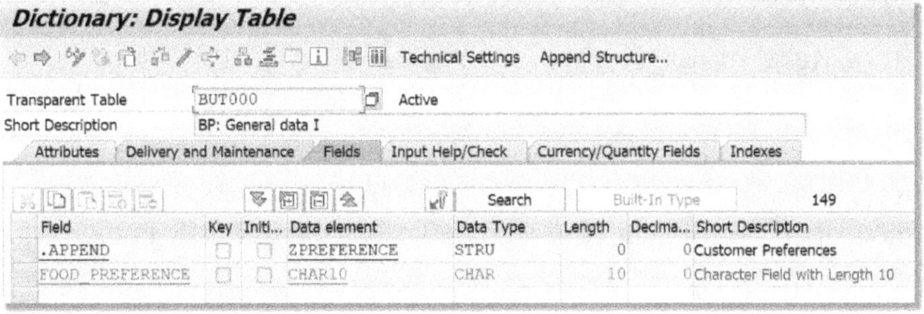

Figure 31: Append custom field to SAP standard table

The new field does not appear in the SAP delivered CDS view. Hence, if this field is required as part of the CDS view then we need to create an extend view. The process for creating an extension view is same as creating any other CDS view. The only difference is that we need to select the Extend view template if we want some code to be generated for us.

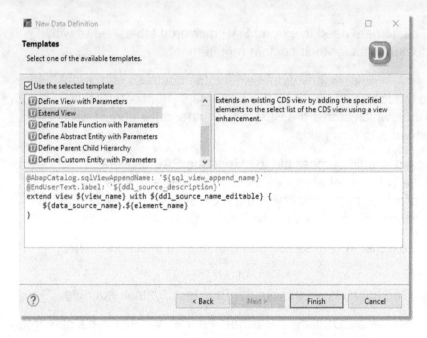

Figure 32: Create new Data definition for Extend View

Sample code for the extend view would be as shown below:

```
@AbapCatalog.sqlViewAppendName: 'ZIBPEXTEND1'
@EndUserText.label: 'BP extend view'
extend view I_BusinessPartner with zi_BP_Extend {
    but000.food_preference as Preference
}
```

Note that all the data sources of the original view can be accessed in the extend view. In our case we can access the new field in the extend view.

Now activate the extend view and run the SAP delivered CDS view (I_BusinessPartner).

You would notice that the new field is part of the output of the SAP view I_BusinessPartner.

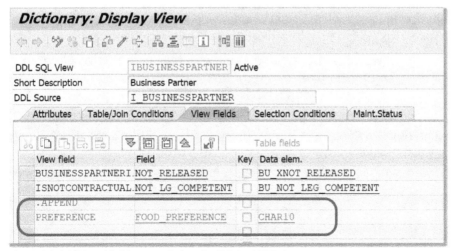

Raw Data

100 rows retrieved - 27 ms (partial result)   SQL Console | Data Aging | Number of Entries

heSearchHelp	BPFirstNameSearchHelp	Preference	IndependentAddressID	IsActiveEntity	BirthDate
	BILL			X	0
	RYAN			X	0
	RYAN			X	0
	TOM			X	0
	DALTON			X	0
	DALTON			X	0
	JOHN			X	0

Figure 33: View with extended fields

If you check the sql view of the original CDS view then you would notice that the new field has been appended to the original view.

As you can see it is very easy to extend the SAP delivered view without any modification. The new fields are appended to the Original CDS view and can also be accessed when reading data from the CDS view in your ABAP program.

Dictionary: Display View

DDL SQL View	IBUSINESSPARTNER Active	
Short Description	Business Partner	
DDL Source	I_BUSINESSPARTNER	

Attributes | Table/Join Conditions | View Fields | Selection Conditions | Maint.Status

Table fields

View field	Field	Key	Data elem.
BUSINESSPARTNERI.NOT_RELEASED		☐	BU_XNOT_RELEASED
ISNOTCONTRACTUAL.NOT_LG_COMPETENT		☐	BU_NOT_LEG_COMPETENT
.APPEND		☐	
PREFERENCE	FOOD_PREFERENCE	☐	CHAR10

Figure 34: Additional fields appended to the Original CDS view

5. Create a List Application with CDS views

In this chapter we will use CDS views and create a UI5 list application to display a list of Sales Orders. We will do this without writing a single line of code in UI5. This would be possible with the use of Fiori Elements for UI5 and CDS annotations. At the end of this exercise our List report will appear as shown below.

Figure 35: Sales Order list application

The application will have the following features:

- The Sales Order data will be shown in a list report.
- It would be possible to search for Sales order with wild card search.
- It would be possible to see the details of the Sales Order in an object page.

The high-level block diagram for the artifacts that we will create is as shown below.

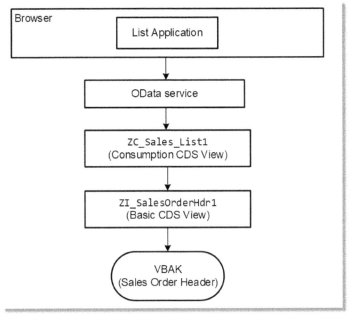

Figure 36: List App high-level block diagram

- The data of the Sales Order is stored in table VBAK. We will be using this table as the base table for selecting the data.
- We will create an interface CDS view to expose the relevant fields from the base table.
- The Consumption CDS view will consume the fields exposed via the Interface CDS view and will be used to add UI and OData annotations.
- The OData service will be created through the CDS OData annotation.
- UI5 List view application will consume the created OData service to display the business partner details.

5.1 Create Interface and Consumption CDS views

Create a new Data Definition for an Interface CDS view to select from Sales Order header table (VBAK).

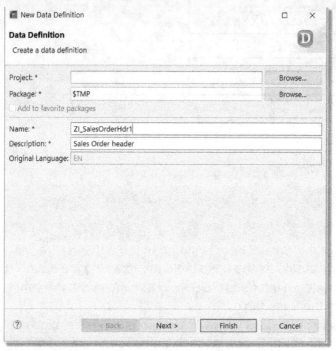

Figure 37: New Data Definition for Interface view

Enter the Name of the Data definition and the Description. The name entered here is the name of the CDS view.

Once done, click on next and select the Transport Request. If the data definition is created in local objects, then click on next.

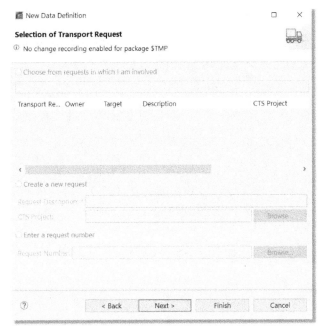

Figure 39: Selection of Transport Request

In the next screen you can use the template. We will use the Define

New Data Definition

Templates

Select one of the available templates.

☑ Use the selected template

Define View	Defines a simple CDS view with one data
Define View with Join	source.
Define View with Association	
Define View with To-Parent Association	
Define View with Parameters	

```
@AbapCatalog.sqlViewName: '${sql_view_name}'
@AbapCatalog.compiler.compareFilter: true
@AbapCatalog.preserveKey: true
@AccessControl.authorizationCheck: #CHECK
@EndUserText.label: '${ddl_source_description}'
define view ${ddl_source_name_editable} as select from ${data_source_name}
    ${cursor}
}
```

< Back   Next >   Finish   Cancel

Figure 38: Select Data definition template

View template.

In the editor we need to change the sqlViewName, enter the table name for select and enter the componets (fields) of the view.

The final code would be as shown below:

```
@AbapCatalog.sqlViewName: 'ZSALESORD1'
@AbapCatalog.compiler.compareFilter: true
@AbapCatalog.preserveKey: true
@AccessControl.authorizationCheck: #CHECK
@EndUserText.label: 'Sales Order header'
define view ZI_SalesOrderHdr1
  as select from vbak
{
  key vbeln as Salesdoc, //Sales Document
  erdat as CreationDate, //Date on Which Record Was Created
  auart as DocType, //Sales Document Type

  @Semantics.amount.currencyCode: 'DocCurrency'
  netwr as NetValue, //Net Value

  @Semantics.currencyCode: true
  waerk as DocCurrency, //SD document currency
  vkorg as SalesOrg, //sales Organization
  vtweg as DistChannel //Distribution Channel
  •  }
```

As you have noticed we have used 2 annotations for the fields in the CDS view.

- `@Semantics.currencyCode: true` : This annotation tells the framework that the field 'DocCurrency' is a currency field. Once this is done, this field can be used as a reference for the amount field.

- `@Semantics.amount.currencyCode:` This annotation is used for amount fields and is used to provide a reference to the currency field. This is not new, and we do the same in the DDIC tables as well. Refer to the below figure to see where it is done for tables.

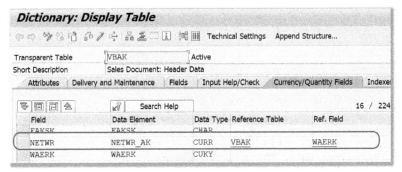

Figure 40: Currency reference for amount fields in Tables

Now you can save and activate the interface view.

Once done, now create a consumption view for the base view. Consumption views are used for adding annotations for the Consumer (in this case our UI5 app).

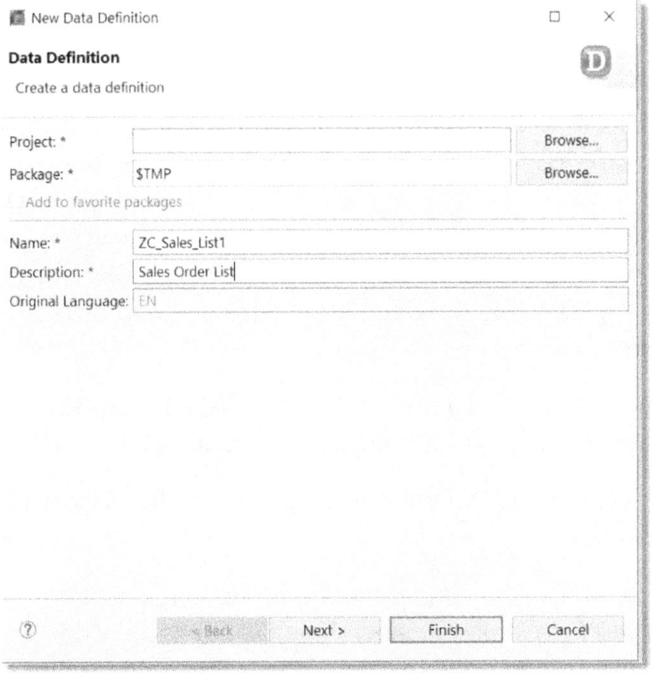

Figure 41: Data Definition for Consumption View

Like the Interface view, enter the Name and Description of the view. In the new screens select the Transport request and then the template.

Once the code is generated, replace the code with the code shown below.

```
@AbapCatalog.sqlViewName: 'ZCSALESLIST1'
@AbapCatalog.compiler.compareFilter: true
@AbapCatalog.preserveKey: true
@AccessControl.authorizationCheck: #CHECK
@EndUserText.label: 'Sales Order List'
define view ZC_Sales_List1
  as select from ZI_SalesOrderHdr1
{
  key Salesdoc,
  CreationDate,
  DocType,

  @Semantics.amount.currencyCode: 'DocCurrency'
  NetValue,

  @Semantics.currencyCode: true
  DocCurrency,
  SalesOrg,
  DistChannel

}
```

The consumption view selects the data from the Interface view. Please note that for components, we use the alias names which we had defined for the fields in the interface view. Now you can save and activate the view.

As you would have noticed, this view is not very different from the interface view as we have not yet added the annotations for the UI.

As a next step let us now add the following annotations for displaying the data in our UI5 app.

- @OData.publish: true: This annotation creates an OData service for the Consumption view. This OData service can then be activated and used in the UI5 app. Please note that Odata service created with this annotation does not create an

OData project and also does not create the MPC_EXT and DPC_EXT classes. This method of creating OData should be used only when there is no need to change the code in the MPC and DPC ext classes.

- `@Search.searchable: true:` Defines if a CDS view or entity is generally relevant for search scenarios. This annotation must be set in case other search-related annotations are being defined for elements of the respective CDS view or entity.

- `@Search.defaultSearchElement: true:` Specifies that the element is to be considered in a freestyle search (for example a SELECT...) where no columns are specified.

- `@Search.fuzzinessThreshold:` Specifies the least level of fuzziness (with regard to some comparison criteria passed at runtime) the element has to have to be considered in a fuzzy search at all.

- `@UI.headerInfo.typeName:` This annotation represents the title of an object page, for example. The element is required and can be omitted only when the @EndUserText.label is specified on view level.

- `@UI.headerInfo.typeNamePlural:` This annotation represents a list title.

- `@UI.lineItem.position:` With This annotation you specify the order of the columns of a list. This annotation is mandatory.

- `@UI.identification.position:` With This annotation you specify the order of entries on the object view floorplan. This annotation is mandatory.

The final code would be as shown below:

```
@AbapCatalog.sqlViewName: 'ZCSALESLIST1'
@AbapCatalog.compiler.compareFilter: true
```

```
@AbapCatalog.preserveKey: true
@AccessControl.authorizationCheck: #CHECK
@EndUserText.label: 'UI5 List report'

@OData.publish: true

@Search.searchable : true
@UI.headerInfo:{ typeName: 'Sales Order List',
typeNamePlural: 'Sales Order List' }

define view ZC_Sales_List1
  as select from ZI_SalesOrderHdr1
{
  @UI.lineItem.position: 10
  @Search: { defaultSearchElement: true,
fuzzinessThreshold: 0.7 }
  @UI.identification.position: 10
  key Salesdoc,

  @UI.lineItem.position: 20
  @UI.identification.position: 20
  CreationDate,

  @UI.lineItem.position: 30
  @Search.defaultSearchElement: true
  @UI.identification.position: 30
  DocType,

  @UI.lineItem.position: 40
  @UI.identification.position: 40
  @Semantics.amount.currencyCode: 'DocCurrency'
  NetValue,

  @UI.lineItem.position: 50
  @UI.identification.position: 50
  @Semantics.currencyCode: true
  DocCurrency,

  @UI.lineItem.position: 60
  @UI.identification.position: 60
  SalesOrg,

  @UI.lineItem.position: 70
  @UI.identification.position: 70
  DistChannel
```

```
}
```

Once the CDS view code is updated, you can save and activate the

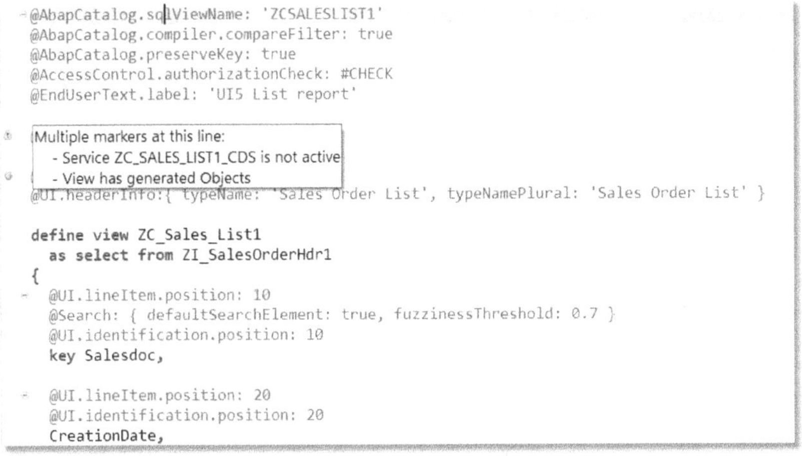

```
@AbapCatalog.sqlViewName: 'ZCSALESLIST1'
@AbapCatalog.compiler.compareFilter: true
@AbapCatalog.preserveKey: true
@AccessControl.authorizationCheck: #CHECK
@EndUserText.label: 'UI5 List report'

Multiple markers at this line:
  - Service ZC_SALES_LIST1_CDS is not active
  - View has generated Objects
@UI.headerInfo:{ typeName: 'Sales Order List', typeNamePlural: 'Sales Order List' }

define view ZC_Sales_List1
  as select from ZI_SalesOrderHdr1
{
   @UI.lineItem.position: 10
   @Search: { defaultSearchElement: true, fuzzinessThreshold: 0.7 }
   @UI.identification.position: 10
   key Salesdoc,

   @UI.lineItem.position: 20
   @UI.identification.position: 20
   CreationDate,
```

Figure 42: Consumption CDS view

view.

Once the CDS view is activated, you can hover the mouse beside the OData annotation and check the name of the created service.

5.2 Activate and Maintain OData service

The next step would be to activate the service via transaction

Figure 43: Activate and Maintain Services

/IWFND/MAINT_SERVICE

In the maintain service transaction, you can create and activate the

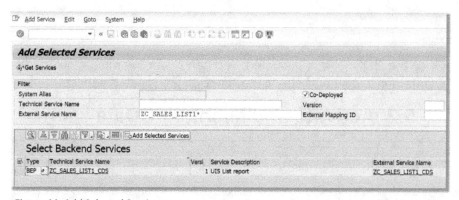

Figure 44: Add Selected Services

service by clicking on the 'Add Service' button.

Search for your service by entering the service name in the field 'External Service Name'. This is the same name which the system displays in the Hana Studio when you hover the mouse beside the OData Service annotation.

The system finds the service and display in the list below. Select the

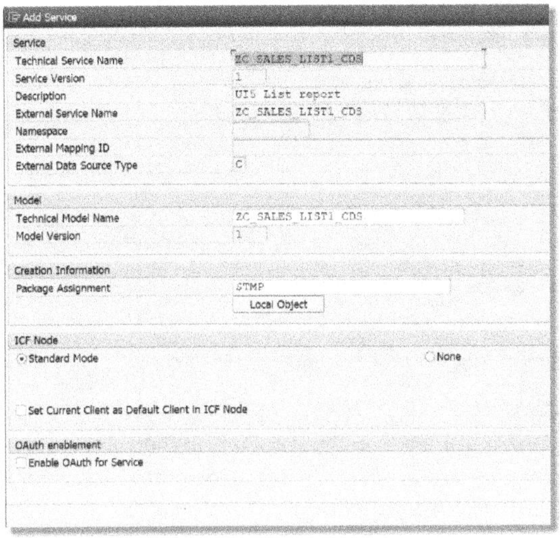

Figure 45: Add Service

service and click on 'Add Selected Services'.

Click on Continue in the Add service popup. The system then activates the service. The service can now be consumed from the UI5 app. Before we start with the UI, it is a good idea to test the service in the Gateway client.

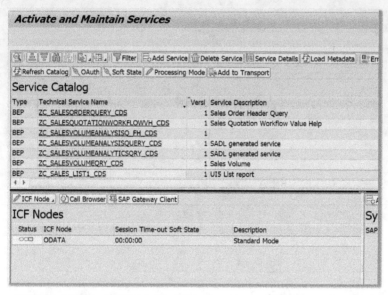

Figure 46: Activate and Maintain service

Select the service and click on 'SAP Gateway Client'. In the gateway client you can execute the Entity set via GET call and retrieve the Sales Order data. Since the Sales order table would normally have a lot of data, you can use the addition '$top=10' to get only 10 records.

Once you get the data from the service, you are ready to start with the UI.

Figure 47: Test service from the Gateway Client

5.3 Create UI5 project

To create a UI5 all, launch the webide and create a new project with

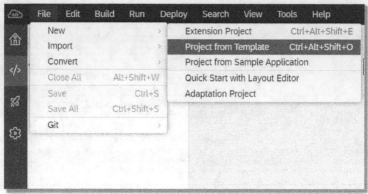

Figure 48: Create Project from Template

template.

Since we are creating a List application, select the 'List Report Application' template.

Figure 50: Select Template

After selecting the template, the wizard prompts you to specify the name and the title.

New List Report Application
Basic Information

Template Selection	Basic Information	Data Connection	Annotation Selection	Template Customization

Project Name*

SalesOrdListReport

App Descriptor Data
Title*

Sales Order list Report

Namespace

Description

Previous   Next

Figure 49: List report basic information

In the following screens you need to specify furter details e.g. Odata service, Annotation files etc. Once all the necessary details are provides the system create a new UI5 project as shown in the screenshot below:

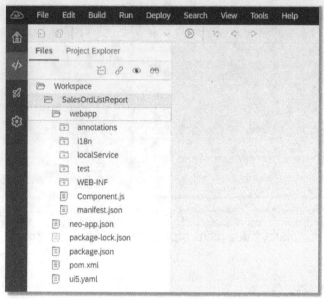

Figure 51: UI5 Project structure

Now you are ready to execute the app, as all the UI code is generated. You can execute the application by selecting the Project and then selecting Run -> Run as SAP Fiori Launchpad Sandbox.

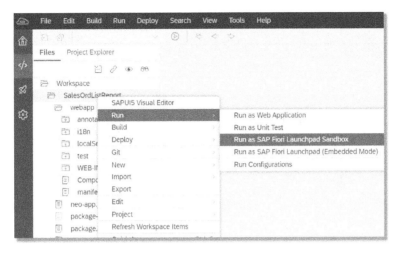

Figure 52: Execute list application

The system opens a new browser session and runs your new application.

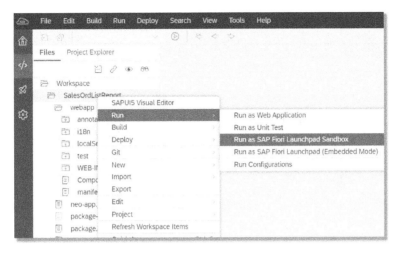

Figure 53: Sales Order list application

As you can see from the above screenshot, the UI5 app is created and ready for use.

If has all the features which we added through the annotation.

- Search for records using wildcards

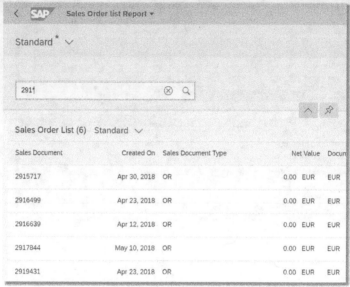

Figure 54: Search for records

- Position of elements as specified via annotation
- Object page for the detail view

SUMMARY

As you can see, we have successfully created a working app with CDS views. The OData and the metadata for the UI was created through the annotations which we specified in the Consumption view. This simply shows the power of CDS views and the direction which SAP wants to take when building new applications.

Appendix

1. Installation of ABAP Development Toolkit

Eclipse is an integrated development environment (IDE) used in computer programming, and is the most widely used Java IDE. It contains a base workspace and an extensible plug-in system for customizing the environment. ABAP development in Eclipse requires ABAP plug-ins.

In this chapter we would go through the installation process and familiarize with the environment. This will set the right base for the rest of the chapters in this book.

Installation

Following steps are involved for setting up the Eclipse development environment.

- Download and Install Eclipse
- Download and Install the Eclipse Plugin for ABAP

development
- Connect the Eclipse to the Backend SAP system.

1.1 Download and Install Eclipse

To download and install Eclipse, please follow the instruction in the below link:

https://tools.hana.ondemand.com/#abap

You could also install Eclipse directly from eclipse.org but it is best to follow the detailed instructions in the provided link.

The link also provides detailed information on Prerequisites of Installation and Installation procedure.

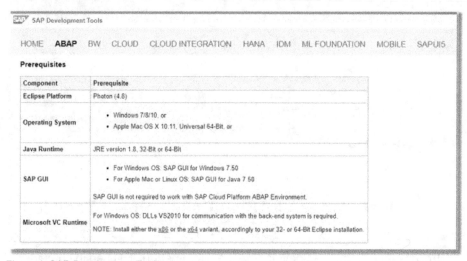

Figure 1: SAP Development Tools

1.2 Install the ABAP Development Tools for SAP NetWeaver (ADT)

Once the Eclipse has been installed, the ABAP Development Plug-ins can be installed from the Eclipse menu bar, select: Help > Install New Software menu option.

Figure 2: Install New Software

In the dialog box add the URL https://tools.hana.ondemand.com/neon (e.g. for Eclipse Neon 4.6).

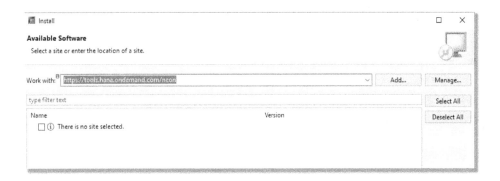

Figure 3: Available Software

Press Enter to display the available features. Select ABAP Development Tools for SAP NetWeaver and click Next.

On the next wizard page, you get an overview of the features to be installed. Click Next.

Confirm the license agreements and click Finish to start the installation

You can switch to the ABAP perspective by clicking the **Open Perspective** button or using the menu: **Window > Open Perspective**.

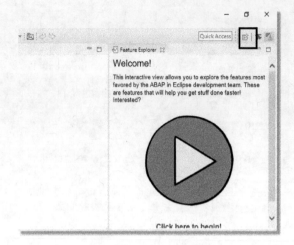

Figure 4: Open Perspective

1.3 Connecting Eclipse to a Backend SAP System

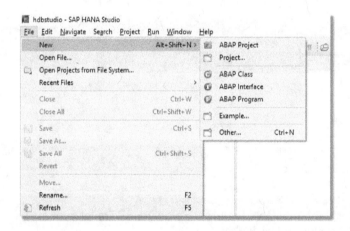

Figure 5: Create New ABAP Project

Once the Eclipse and ABAP Development Plug-ins are installed, we are ready to connect to a SAP backend system. To connect, choose the menu path - File –> New -> ABAP Project.

All the systems from your SAP Logon pad are listed in the next dialog box. Choose and provide the credentials with the client information to login and fetch the technical development objects.

Now the system is added on the left panel and this can now be expanded to navigate to the development package. It is also possible to add the development package as a Favorite package.

More books from Mark

ABAP in S/4HANA	

This book is available in both eBook and Paperback formats. | ABAP in S/4 Hana is a path into the New ABAP programming world. It covers the major building blocks of S/4 Hana like Core Data Services, OData and BOPF.
The book provides good explanation of the concepts with sample code and serves a complete guide for an ABAPer looking forward to learning and building new Application on S/4 Hana.

It also has a dedicated chapter which provides step-by-step guide to building a new application, right from creating a new tables, creating CDS views and exposing the object via Odata service.
It is a must have book for a developer/architect who want to understand the the building blocks of development in S/4 Hana world. |
| eBook
https://www.amazon.com/dp/B07L7DP8HR
Paperback:
https://www.amazon.com/ABAP-S-Hana-Mark-Anderson/dp/1790975964/ref=tmm_pap_swatch_0?_encoding=UTF8&qid=&sr= | |

ABAP Gateway and OData

This book is available in both **eBook** and **Paperback** formats.

The book covers the concepts and process of creating OData services.

Chapter 1 and 2 introduces you to Gateway and OData, and Chapters 3 and 4 describe the process of creating the OData service in detail.

Following different ways of Service creation is covered as part of this book:

- ABAP Code-based implementation
- Service generation via RFC/BOR interface
- Service generation through CDS Consumption views
- Service generation through CDS Annotation @Odata.publish
- Extending an existing OData service

eBook
https://www.amazon.com/dp/B07ZFW5KL9
Paperback:
https://www.amazon.com/SAP-Gateway-OData-Mark-Anderson/dp/1701489546/ref=tmm_pap_swatch_0?_encoding=UTF8&qid=&sr

New ABAP Language features in ABAP 7.4 and 7.5

This book introduces the new ABAP language features of ABAP 7.4 and 7.5. This includes new commands and constructs and examples which are required for developing in the new ABAP world.

The book has good number of ABAP code examples which helps the reader understand the constructs easily. It is a good guide for both a seasoned ABAPer and a ABAP Newbie.

This book is available in both **eBook** and **Paperback** formats.

eBook:
https://www.amazon.com/dp/B07QX1DRGQ

Paperback:
https://www.amazon.com/New-ABAP-Language-features-7-4/dp/1075617472/ref=tmm_pap_swatch_0?_encoding=UTF8&qid=&sr=

Comprehensive SAP ABAP Interview Questions and Answers

This book covers the most important and frequently asked questions in ABAP technical interview. This book aims to help the readers in their SAP interviews.

It covers the following areas:
- ABAP General
- Data Dictionary
- BDC
- Screen Programming
- Forms
- Reports
- ABAP OO
- Performance Tuning
- Interfaces

This book is available in both **eBook** and **Paperback** formats.

eBook:
https://www.amazon.com/dp/B07QX1DRGQ

Paperback:
https://www.amazon.com/dp/109687380X